DO YOU

Keonda Crawley

ISBN: 9781735487151

Printed in the United States of America

Story Corner Publishing Inc.

1510 Atlanta Ave.

Portsmouth, VA 23704

Storycornerpublishing@yahoo.com

Dedication

This book is dedicated to my mom, dad, and sister. Thanks mom and dad for believing in me and always motivating me to follow my dreams. I never thought in a million years I would be writing a book. It was a long time coming, but it is finally here. Mom and dad, your strength and love never goes unnoticed. I hope I make you proud! I love both of you so much.

To my sister, you know I love you with all my heart. I hope I made you proud. You are my motivation that helps me keep moving forward and not give up when the world is cruel to me. You are my sunshine on the rainy days. We are bonded forever! I love you!

This book is also dedicated to all my extended family, grandmothers, aunt and uncle. I love you all. Thank you for your love and support!

TABLE OF CONTENTS

Introduction

Most people know me by my nickname "Kiki." They do not know that my first name is Keonda. People just view me as a girl with cerebral palsy that walks with crutches, but there is much more to me than just this disability. Most people that know me would describe me as a funny, happy, and positive person who is always smiling. They do not know the pain, anger, and frustration that I carry inside my heart. People look at me and say you are so strong; I do not know how you do it. I just reply and say it is not easy because I have been living with cerebral palsy my entire life. However, the truth is, I want to give up every day, but I cannot.

I am the type of person that does not like to ask for help, even if I need help. I do not like the idea, that people think they need to help me only because I have a disability. I usually take my time to figure out how to do something before I ask for help. I try to be strong, but it often gets tough. I live by this quote, "GOD gives His toughest battles to His strongest soldiers." I know God gave me the strength to always push through so I could be an inspiration to others. In God is where I find my strength. I could not take a step forward in any direction without Him. Without God, I am nothing! I cannot accomplish strength on my own because I would have given up a long time ago. It is not easy to endure, but it is necessary. I will continue to live by God's word, pray, and endure like a good soldier. In God's timing my prayers will come to pass because He hears me. In this book, I will show you what enduring and overcoming the hinderances of cerebral palsy look like. Cerebral palsy will not paralyze me!

Chapter 1

Going the Extra Mile

Chapter 1
Going the Extra Mile

L iving with cerebral palsy is something I had to deal with since I was born. Every day is a new learning experience for me.

Somethings can be a little overwhelming because I feel as if I always must go the extra mile to prove myself to someone, and sometimes that can be frustrating and annoying.

I feel like a lot of people do not know how to treat people with disabilities. People usually do not know how to start or hold a conversation with me. I wish there were a class people could take to learn how to deal with people who have disabilities. I believe everyone should be informed because we should not be treated differently. I get tired of explaining myself and I am sure others like me are tired as well. Half of the time I do not know what goes on with my body and trying to explain it to someone else is so frustrating!

Cerebral palsy (CP) is a group of disorders that affect a person's ability to move and maintain balance and posture. CP is the most common motor disability in childhood. Cerebral means having to do with the brain. Palsy means weakness or problems with using the muscles. Symptoms include exaggerated reflexes, floppy or rigid limbs, and involuntary motions. These appear by early childhood. Long-term treatment includes physical and other therapies, drugs, and sometimes surgery.

I tell people I am normal just like them and to treat me as such. I just may do things at a slower rate, but I can do mostly everything the next person can. I have limitations, but I still manage. I cannot keep my balance on my own, so I use crutches to help me walk, but I do not allow that to discourage me. I do not have to use my crutches in the house because everything is within reach. I only need them when I am out and about.

Sometimes I wish people would see me as "normal" without me having to convince them. That is my greatest desire. I look at my sister sometimes and wish I knew how it felt to just get up and walk and not have to worry about getting my crutches or needing more time to get myself together. To walk without restrictions is what I pray for most. Honestly, I get a little jealous sometimes because I wish I had the ability to switch bodies or even switch places. How come I must be the one that has to work extra hard at life? It might sound crazy to some people until life happens and it does not turn out the way you expected it to be. I try to allow my perspective to change about my situation, but I just revert backwards once I see someone doing what I wish I could. I would get upset going the extra mile to do physical therapy, surgery, and dealing with braces placed on my legs. I just want to walk like my sister. We came from the same womb, so how is it that I got cheated? I love my sister, but I just have so many questions. Why was I born with cerebral palsy?

I had to learn to cope with all these thoughts and even how to love myself better. It is a process and sometimes I take steps backwards. I began to feel sad and depressed at times. How do I overcome this? I get tired of going the extra mile to do things that just come natural to most. I value most things people take for granted because I know what it is like to not have it, like perfectly functioning legs to walk. I must go the extra mile in everything I do like making friends, relationships, getting a job, going to school, etc.

remember my dad and I going to see our pastor to talk about my frustration finding a job. Our pastor suggested that I explain to employers how I maneuvered around Norfolk State University (NSU) to receive my bachelor's and master's degree. I was thinking to myself in that moment why do I always have to go the "extra mile" to prove myself to people who could probably never survive walking a day in my shoes. I wanted to tell our pastor I am tired of proving myself to people, but I took in what he was saying because it was incredibly good advice about life. I just felt like I had enough with proving myself to people, but that does not mean I am giving up on myself. I just know what I want out of life and I will not settle. I feel numb to a lot of things and I have these empty voids that need to be filled, so focusing on irrelevant things are just a waste of time. I am tired! Proving myself over and over just tears down the little hope I try to hold on to. Now I must prove myself for a job? Some people working in these jobs do not even know what they are doing, but they got hired with no problem. Are you serious? Oh, but I must prove myself, and most times they shut the door on me without even giving me a chance. It really makes me angry to even think about it!

I find myself shutting down often just to cope with life. My "safe place" is my room, so I spend a lot of time there. When I am there, I can let my hair down and be myself without anyone judging me. When I go out into the world, I am constantly wearing my game face and working extra hard just to measure up. I do not have to do all of that in my safe place. In fact, I do not even have to deal with people period when I am in my room. That is always a plus for me, but the downfall is when I do go out. I sometimes have anxiety and find it hard to socialize.

I do have friends and cousins that I am comfortable around and I can just be myself. It feels good to spend time with them. I am also amazingly comfortable around my sister. She is literally my best friend. I think she is an angel sent by God, because I could not imagine my life without her. We have so much fun together. She understands me and I am not judged by her. I am grateful for my friends because they accept me for who I am. I love my cousins and consider them my best friends as well. I enjoy having them around. A lot of people do not know my daily struggles because they do not walk in my shoes. I could do all the explaining in the world, but at the end of the day some people just will not understand, and I have learned to be ok with it.

Overall, I learn more ways how to cope with myself every day because I am truly blessed and just wish somethings were different in my life. There are times when things still bother me, and I do not know why. I believe every day I become a stronger person because of all the stuff I have been through and have not given up yet! I have gained patience and endurance over time so I can handle things a little better than the next person. Things that might break one person like being talked about, do not bother me. I have been criticized all my life, so I am used to it now. I have heard countless jokes about how I walk, how my legs and feet look, and the fact that I must use leg braces and crutches to get around. Those comments use to make me feel bad, but now I know it is just building my character. I know that the people joking about me would not last a day in my shoes. The fact that I must go the extra mile all the time would exhaust them. I even get tired of going the extra mile, but I cannot just trade myself in for someone different. I must deal with my limitations every single day. It takes courage to be me.

I used to wonder what my life would be like without cerebral palsy, but of course I will never know, and it is ok now. I know that cerebral palsy does not make me who I am. I am "ME." I just wish people could see me for who I am instead of tuning me out. Sometimes I want to scream, "Do You SEE ME?"

Chapter 2

Staying True to Yourself

Chapter 2
Stay True to Yourself

Most of my life I have tried to be someone other than myself. I would follow the latest trends to stay up to date with what everyone else was doing. I even tried to dress different to fit in with the crowd. I always wanted to belong and to be noticed. I wanted attention. I allowed society to put me in a box and have me hating myself. Social media adds more pressure to fit the mode that society built. The picture of myself started to get blurry in middle school and by high school my true self was gone. Now that I am older, I realize that during those years in school I did not stay true to myself. I did not love myself like I should have. I wasted time trying to be something that I was not. I would look up to the popular kids in school and get caught up in trying to act like them, hoping that I would get the acknowledgment that they did. I wanted the attention that everyone showed them. Not realizing that some people loved me just the way I am.

I must remember that I am a child of GOD and that I am fearfully & wonderfully made. He really created me perfect just the way I am, but I must believe that for myself every day. I am getting to know me more and more every day. Staying true to myself matters to me now. Who am I? What are the things I enjoy? I am someone with a heart of gold and I would help anyone in need. I am a loyal sister, cousin, daughter, and friend and they are blessed to have me in their lives. I am not being prideful or boasting, I just know I have a heart for people because I know what it is like to need someone. I know that I am one of kind and that nobody can walk in my shoes and live my life.

I am family oriented and I do not go out a lot. You will not find me in clubs, bars, etc. I love being home watching tv shows on *Netflix* and *Hulu*. I love watching reality tv such as Real Housewives of Atlanta, Teen Mom, New York Black Ink Crew, and Black Ink Crew Chicago. I spend most of my time in the house because it is the place I do not have to pretend. I love looking up new music and listening to music. Music is like therapy to me because it calms me down and makes me feel good. My favorite artists are Bow Wow, Omarion, Drake, Ashanti and many more.

I love to write poetry and express how I am feeling on paper. I have found writing to be a peaceful getaway for me. Writing has always been something that I genuinely enjoy because I feel that it helps me when I am feeling down. It helps me to heal from pain I accumulated over the course of a day. Writing is part of my healing process. I can express my emotions in a healthy manner. I sometimes have a hard time speaking my truth and getting my thoughts out. I am working on this every day. I also try to be as selfless as possible. I love to see other people happy. I do not like to see other people hurt because I have been there too many times myself. I push myself every day because I am afraid to fail.

To be honest, I fear what the future holds for me because I do not want to fail at anything I propose to do. I am comfortable with just allowing someone else to take control of the decision regarding my life. I do not want to mess up anything. I am working on my confidence so I can believe in myself more. I know at some point in my life I will have to make my own decisions. I must take control of fear instead of it controlling me. I know fear holds me back from living my life and doing things that make me happy. I have goals and dreams. I want to one day ook over my life and be pleased with all the accomplishments I have completed. I feel like my 30th birthday is around the corner, so I must get a move on things once I stop being afraid. I am afraid of failing things I have not even tried. It is all in the thought for me. I also want to get married and start a family. I want to know what it is like to be loved, feel joy, and to be happy. I fear that I will be 40 years old with no love life or children of my own. My biggest fear is ending up alone, so I stop getting my hopes up and try not to think about it as much.

A friend that I know longer associate with, told me on many occasions that I was going to live alone. When I tell you that it hurt me to hear that, trust me it hurt! I tried to throw it out of my mind, but it only pushed the seed of fear deeper into my mind. I wonder if what they say is true sometimes. I pray that it is not, but the way my life goes some days I do not know. I feel like the chances of that happening increase a little because of the fact I have cerebral palsy, but I do not allow that to stop me. I tell people all the time if they want to get to know me, they must accept the fact that I come with the baggage of cerebral palsy. Of course, if I could change it I would, but I cannot. So, it is a package deal that they sign up for. My point is, I want to live life without fear one day. I would truly be heartbroken if I had to live life alone. I know GOD's timing is always the perfect timing and I shall receive my blessings on time. I have patience and will wait for the perfect career opening, the perfect home to purchase, and the perfect husband to start a family with. Everyone might not want the life that I want and that is fine, but I am ready for the desires of my heart.

Chapter 3

Feeling Like a Burden

Chapter 3
Feeling Like A Burden

Something that has been weighing heavy on me is feeling like a burden to my whole family. It makes me feel sad because I have seen all the money my mom and dad have put into my surgeries, physical therapy, and braces for my legs. I feel that if I were "normal" that they would not have to stress so much concerning me. I wish I were "normal" like my sister and did not have to worry about cerebral palsy, but the fact is I must deal with this every day. It is not curable, although I pray every day for a medical breakthrough. Until then, it will not just disappear! It is a part of who I am, and I am trying to deal with it every day.

I feel I burden my sister the most because I depend on her a lot. She is the one that would come to my rescue the most. She is literally my right hand and I love her for it. I am afraid that when she starts to live her own life, I will lose her. I know one day she will get a job, find a soulmate, and maybe even have children, so my days of help from her are numbered. It might sound silly to you, but I do not know what I would do without her. I do want her to be able to live her own life without worrying about me, so I try my best to bother her as little as possible. I try not to burden her with my problems. She really does make the best of helping me, and I do not know if she knows how much she means to me. I really appreciate her! We hang out together all the time, but I have always wondered if she gets tired of dragging me along. It makes me feel uncomfortable sometimes because although she is my sister, I think I should have more stuff to do and maybe other people to hang with. I do not want her to regret me or have resentment towards me in the future because she has spent so much of her time including me in her schedule. I do not want her worrying about me at all if it adds more stress on her. I want her to have her own life that does not include me tagging along, even if it involves me spending some time alone or exploring getting to know new people. I would have to step out of my comfort zone so the fear of new people in my life will not consume me. I do not have many close friends. I can count them on one hand, hence why my sister is my go-to. I need friends that understand me and share the same interest. I like going to plays, musicals, concerts, movies, nice restaurants, and taking girl trips.

To be honest, I distance myself from my few friends and family because I feel incomplete. I feel as if I am plain or boring and that no one would want to be around me anyway. Everyone I know have interesting things going on with them such as significant others &/or children. I am not saying you must have a spouse and children to be interesting, but at least they have families to keep them occupied with fun things to do.

Things have changed between the ones I use to spend time with and myself because of our priorities and responsibilities. We live in two different worlds now, so it is hard to relate to them. We are adults now walking different paths in life and theirs do not cross mines as much as it used to. I guess it is ok because that means less people to "burden." I am in this in between phase in life where I am just trying to understand myself and purpose in detail without going crazy. I know my family and friends love me and do not think I am a burden, but sometimes I do feel that way. Taking the necessary step to make new friends is where I am. It is scary, but I think I should make the effort to give my sister a break. I know I had a lot of opportunity to make friends in college, but I just did not think it was important then. I had one good friend and thought I was good until our priorities changed. New chapters in life are sometimes good, although I wish I would have made other friends in college so I could have a variety to choose from at times like this. I regret not being more outspoken and willing to hang out more with other people. Do not get me wrong, I did hang out with other people in college and I met some amazing individuals, but I only opened up to one. I allowed myself to be consumed with just hanging out with my best friend at that time. I did not give myself the full opportunity to let other people in my life. I shut the door before they could even get to know me. Fear has me rejecting others before they could reject me. They could be a nice person, but I will never know if I do not get over the fear of rejection. So, that is nobody's fault but mine and I have learned my lesson. I cannot go back and change the past; I just must keep moving forward.

Maybe once I figure out my purpose in life, I will not have the same battles I deal with daily. I will not feel lonely, depressed, insecure, rejected, or abandoned. Only God knows what the future holds for me, so I have some soul searching to do. I do know I do not want to be a burden, be alone, or forgotten. I have seen what it looks like with seniors who do not have family to depend on and it breaks my heart. I do not want to simply exist; I want to live an abundant life full of joy! Life is too short, and I take a stand against fear today.

Chapter 4

Depression

Chapter 4
Depression

There were plenty of days where I thought I was better off dead than living another day. Suicide was on my mind and it was hard to shake. At times I feel unloved and invisible. Some days are better than others. I even found it hard to love myself for who I was because I was always wishing to be someone else. High school is when I allowed my thoughts to get the best of me.

Suicidal thoughts use to chase me down to the point of trying to figure out ways to accomplish it. The only thing that stopped me was the thought of feeling pain, and I was too afraid to go through with it. My biggest downfall is not believing in myself. I let other people tell me who I was and what I was going to be in the future. When in reality, I am the author of my life and I have the right to create my own story. Of course, God has the final say, no one else should.

My four years in high school were a roller coaster ride. I had low days dealing with sadness and depression, and happy days when I felt good about myself. I never knew what type of day I was going to have. My mood was always up and down. Walking the school halls not feeling accepted and seeing a division among the other students. There was a popular section and an unpopular section. Of course, I fell in the unpopular section, but to me, I was in the invisible section. Maybe I made up that section all alone, at least that is how I felt. I even hate using the words popular and unpopular; it makes no sense to me. But the reality is, these words exist, and they have meaning that manifested every day for me in high school. I felt like I was not a part of the school, even though I had a small group of friends that I hung out with.

I even had a crush on this boy in high school, and I really wanted him to notice me, but that did not happen. I just felt like he kind of dismissed me and did not think twice about me. He was a popular football player and I wanted to be noticed by him. Crazy, right? I think that was the craziest thought I had in my head back in high school.

I allowed people to bring me down with their comments about me. A lot of my classmates made jokes about me, especially the boys in the classroom. The joking really brought my spirit down and made me more depressed. I just do not understand why people have so many jokes and things to say about me. I am a nice person. Most of the boys were rude and immature in high school, and I hated being in the classroom with them sometimes. My thoughts were, "Please grow up! Everything can't be that funny!"

Dating was also a thing in high school that depressed me. I used to have to sit and watch others linking up and there was no link for me. When it came to me, there was always a missing link. I wanted a boyfriend like the others but was not privileged to have one. This was a hard pill to swallow for me because I did not think that would consume me the way it did. I got jealous of others not even knowing if they were happy or not. I just know I was not happy. I felt as if I was not good enough to even hang around the way I was avoided, and it pissed me off a lot. I would go from sad to angry.

I allowed depression to really get the best of me and I started cutting my wrist in high school. It was a very dark place in my life, and I wish I could go back and not have done that to myself. I just remember the marks I would have on my wrist. I would cover up my wrist with long sleeves and bracelets so that people would not see the marks. I was not in my right mind set, and I allowed what people said about me and the jokes get the best of me. I was a mess during my high school years. I was really looking for approval, attention, and love in all the wrong places from all the wrong people. I look back at the things I put myself through and I realize I wasted time worrying about what my peers thought of me. If only I knew then what I know now, I think I would be further along mentally and emotionally.

When my parents found out that I was cutting myself, they took me to seek help. I started therapy to talk about my issues surrounding depression. Therapy got me over the hurdle of cutting my wrist. I learned how to *cope* with depression in a better way. High school was a nightmare for me, and I am glad that it is finally over! By the way, I had a much better experience in college. I feel that high school had a lot of immature vain people that thought they would be popular forever.

Well, news flash the tables do turn, and I am glad they did not turn for the worse involving me. Real life is no joke! I see some of those people who used to make fun of me, and they look a hot mess. I feel bad for them. Even some of the boys that use to pick on me are asking me out on dates, but they can save it because back then they did not want me, now I am hot they all on me.

Ha-ha. They fill up my social media DM like they forgot about what they use to call me. It really confuses me half the time. If only I could have foreseen all this then! I would have never been so hard on myself thinking I was not good enough when in fact, I was overqualified. I see my peers on social media and I see the struggle and heartache that some of them are dealing with. High school did not prepare us for the real world nor the challenges that were ahead of us. I see the popular transition to the not so popular, and ones that were healthy now have disabilities. I see some single with multiple kids and others on drugs dealing with depression. Half of the peers I know, are still looking for a decent job/career in life. So, at the end of the day, what I went through in high school was not even a glimpse of what real life is.

My point is, do not ever let people bring you down and tell you that you are less than. Who are they to tell you who you can and cannot be in life? I wish I would not have put so much pressure on myself in high school and tried to conform to what society thought I should be doing in life. High school is just a chapter in your life. It is not the end, so I had to turn the page and quickly. There is so much more to life than high school drama. People are just people, and I had to get delivered from people. We are all just trying to figure out life in our own way. Just live your life to the best of your ability, because ten years from now the problems you worried about then will be irrelevant and will not even matter. It is all just a bunch of nonsense anyway. Ha-ha. When I was younger, I thought my problems were the end of the world, but now I know that was far from the case. Be the best *YOU* that you can be! Remember that you have a purpose in life that only you can fulfill.

The Present

I still deal with depression until this day. It has never really gone away. I have only covered it up with other things to pass the time. It comes in as rushing waves sometimes. I would feel good one moment, and the next I would be really low. This depression followed me to college. Although college was much easier than high school, I still had a hard time coping. The people in college really did not care that I had cerebral palsy and walked with crutches. It all kind of caught me off guard because I was prepared to hear all the jokes. Norfolk State University was a different experience all together. The people really got to know me for who I was, and it was refreshing to say the least. I almost felt a since of normalcy in my life while I was there.

I did have days where I would cry to myself because I felt lonely. Away from home, surrounded by strangers. There were days when I would just lay in the bed and just listen to music all day. I was too depressed to even get out the bed. I had some tough days that I wish I could forget. Anxiety would even get the best of me, and once that happened, the day was over for me. I would be in a sad mood and would not be able to come out of it until the next day. I put such a high standard on myself that at more times than not, I failed to meet it. I gave myself such a hard time. I am my own worst enemy.

I do believe going to Norfolk State University made me become a stronger person, despite my meltdowns. I had to learn how to speak up for myself and to become independent. When I tell you, I went through some trials and tribulations at NSU, you better believe I did! I had to get use to expressing how I felt because those people would chew you up and spit you out. I hate confrontation and dealing with people, so this was a journey for me. I had to work my way through that. Trust me; I am still learning until this day.

I learned to not allow stuff to bother me as much. I became more carefree and began doing things that I wanted to do. When I was in college, I eventually learned how to go to different events by myself. A lot of people would come up to me and ask was I eating alone. They would wonder why I was not with anyone. Most of the people that questioned me said they would have a hard time eating by themselves, or that they simply could not go out by themselves. I can relate, but if I had to wait on someone to hang out or eat dinner with me all the time, I would be at a standstill in life. I think being by myself forced me to be a stronger person, because my friends could not go everywhere with me. I had to navigate on my own. I could not depend on my friends to always be there. I had to be there for myself. Now, I feel like I can go most places by myself and not think anything of it. I do not know if that is a good or bad thing. Ha-ha.

Chapter 5

Experiences at NSU

Chapter 5
Experiences At NSU

Getting prepared for college was an extremely exciting time for me. I was nervous and scared at the same time because this was going to be the first time I was going to be away from home. The whole experience of getting my things ready, placing them in the truck, and arriving at Norfolk State University to see the dorm room that I would be staying in was beyond anything I could ever imagined. A lot of people counted me out, but the fact that I made it to this point in life made me proud of myself for the first time. I could not believe that time flew so fast! I was ready to experience college life and prayed that it would be all I ever dreamed it would be. My Freshman dorm was Called Midrise.

Midrise was an honor's dorm where only honor students could enroll. I worked ridiculously hard in school just to be an honor student so that I could enroll in the honor's dorm. In the honor's dorm, you get more privileges than the regular dorms like less people assigned to a room. I remember walking into the dorm with my mom and seeing all the students signing in and getting their room key. I then signed in to get all the information I needed, and I received my room key. I think that was one of the happiest moments of my life. Freedom!!!! I was really walking into adulthood and could not believe it. When I entered my dorm room, I was able to see my side of the room and I immediately saw how I wanted to decorate it. I was excited beyond words. I made up my bed and put up my things. I did not see my roommate the first night I stayed in the dorm, but she did have a sign up on her side of the room that welcomed me as her roommate. I thought that was so nice of her. I really did feel welcomed.

First Year of College

First day of class, I was super excited and nervous. I woke up extra early just to get ready. I took a shower, put on my clothes, and did my hair. I grabbed my books and class schedule as I walked out the door, placing them in my bookbag. I walked to my first class, which was Biology because I did not know my way around the shuttle stops. I did not want to risk being late. It took me some time, but I got there. So many thoughts were racing through my mind. I was just hoping this class was like nothing I had ever seen before. I did not want to sit in high school all over again. I figured since I was going to be around new people, I should have a new experience. I held onto that hope.

I was nervous to figure things out on my own because I usually had my mom helping me. I had to be ok with being on my own at that point, but I knew I could handle it if I just believed I could do it on my own. Small steps are what I took to get through. As I walked anxiety began to crawl up my back. Anxiety made it hard for me to be around a group of people and especially the ones I did not know. I would feel so out of place. I made it to class, and it was not as bad as I thought it would be. I survived and I did not feel as if all eyes were on me. I also remember having to stand in a long line in the cafeteria the first day of school. The line was so long that it touched the back door of the lunchroom. As I stood in the line, I was thinking to myself about a way I could ask someone for help carrying my food to the table. I got so scared that I froze up. I just kept rehearsing what I was going to say, then an older lady that worked in the cafeteria saw me and told me to come to the front of the line where she would help me. People were looking like, why is she skipping the line? As I think about it now, I laugh to myself. At that moment it was not funny. It was a lot for me to handle then. The lunch lady asked what I wanted to eat, and she got me my favorite meal which was a chicken sandwich and fries. There were so many people in the cafeteria, so I just picked anywhere to sit because the tables were filling quickly. I just sat at a table with a couple of girls. I remember them looking at me like, who is she? I just told them I had nowhere else to sit, I was a freshman, and it was my first day. After that, they did not think anything of me sitting at the table with them.

Once I left the cafeteria, I went back to my dorm room to take a nap because that day wore me out. I still had the room to myself because my roommate had not yet returned. I remember sitting there worried about how I would make it on my own. I ended up crying myself to sleep because I felt so alone. Doing things on my own was a whole new experience for me. It was tough and took some getting used to.

The Bookstore

I remember when I had to get all my books for my first year of classes. I had to stand in another long line waiting to get assistance locating my books. It was torture, but I am glad the clerk was nice. I had to end up asking her if she could carry my books to the register for me. I waited in that line for another twenty minutes just to pay for the books! Once it was finally my turn, all I remember looking at was the total amount for my books and I still did not have them all! The amount was over 500 dollars. I was upset that I had to buy them all and could not even rent them.

When I was ready to leave the register, I had to think fast because I still had books to carry. I ended up putting them all in my book bag at the register, but it took me a little time, so I was holding up the line. I felt embarrassed because everyone was waiting on me. My book bag was so heavy! After waiting on the shuttle bus for thirty minutes, I could not wait to get back to my dorm room. I made it all in one piece but was tired as ever, so I called it a day. Ha-ha.

Getting Through the First Year

I learned a lot over the course of my first year of college. My first semester was a rough experience because it was a lot to get used to. I considered it my breaking in time. Everything was new, plus I had to do things alone. The second half of the year I ended up moving out of Midrise honor's dorm and moved to Rosa Hall dorm. That was a cool dorm. I met some interesting people. I started feeling more independent and I even learned how to do things on my own with ease. It was hard work, but it helped me to figure out the campus better. I also learned how to study better for my classes as well, because the first semester almost wore me out. I eventually adapted to eating and hanging out alone.

The Roommate Experience

Midrise Dorm

My first semester at Midrise Honors dorm I did not see my roommate very much. I grew to be okay with it because it gave me space to figure out who I was on a deeper level. I had privacy and that made it more comfortable. My roommate was a Junior, so she had passed all the freshmen stuff to worry about like making friends with strangers. She had a social life outside of class, unlike me. She was always out with her boyfriend or her friends. So, I pretty much had the room to myself. Even though it was nice to have the room to myself, it got boring sometimes. I did not have anyone to talk to, so I started to look for events on social media or ask people around the campus. I guess I did not really get a sense of the whole roommate experience. I understood the dorm life, but not so much the roommates.

Rosa Hall Dorm

My first roommate in Rosa Hall dorm was a cheerleader for the NSU basketball team. She seemed nice and pretty chill in the very beginning. She was always hanging out and just never seemed to be in the room. At this point, I was used to being alone, so I had a routine down pat. I would go to class, lunch, do homework, go to dinner, and then watch tv until I fell asleep. I still had a desire to make friends, I just had not found anyone that I could truly call a friend. I had known a lot of people, but they were just considered "associates." I wanted more! I wanted someone I could always hang out with and have my best interest in mind. I tried to be open to my roommate to see if we could form a friendship, but things just got weird. During the middle of the semester, I realized that things between her and I were not going to flourish into a friendship because she blocked off her side of the room. She rearranged her tall dresser so I could not see her side of the room at all. I guess that was her way of saying she did not want to be friends. It made me sad a little because of the extreme route that she took, but I got over it. We eventually stopped communicating with each other all together for the remainder of the semester. I do not know what happened, but I feel as if she just wanted her own space in the dorm. I wish she would have just communicated that to me, or whatever it was. I would have had no problem giving her the space. I pray it was not because she was ashamed to be in the same room with me. I am used to people blowing me off because they do not want to be seen with me because of my cerebral palsy. I eventually just moved on from the situation and tried not to think about it. I am telling you, dealing with roommates can be a never-ending rollercoaster ride.

Sophomore Year Roommate

The roommate I had for my second semester as a sophomore, was the coolest one of all. She never treated me differently because of my disability. She really cared and treated me as a friend. We always hung out and had fun. We had girl talks before we went to sleep. She was funny and always had me laughing. It was refreshing to have a roommate that was down to earth and cool to chill with. It was never any drama with her, and that is what I liked the most about her.

Junior Year Roommate

I had a couple of roommates my junior year in college. I had a friend fill out a dorm form to see if we could be in a room together and thank God it worked out. I ended up getting two roommates for the price of one, but it all worked out better than I thought. I was grateful that they wanted to be around after everyone else turned away. They had been roommates before I even came along, and we all became each other's best friends my junior year. We had so much fun together. We would stay up all night having girl talks. I felt like we were always the loudest in our dorm, laughing until 3 o'clock in the morning. Ha-ha.

With three girls in the room, you can imagine all that went on. We enjoyed hanging around each other, but at times we needed space alone. Our moods would clash with each other sometimes. Those were the days I would leave to explore the campus a little more. There was no real privacy in the dorm room and we barely had any space to walk around. It was tight, but we expected that with three people in one tiny room. I remember I used to never want to go home on the weekends because we always had plans to go to the movies, out to eat, and the mall. I had the best adventures with the two of them together. I remember we would ride the Norfolk tide bus to the mall. We would walk from Rosa dorm hall to the Norfolk tide bus to catch a ride to the mall. It was a workout for me with all the walking, but I genuinely enjoyed the memories I had with those ladies.

Senior Year Roommate

I moved back in Midrise honors dorm the first semester of my senior year. I roomed with a girl that soon became a friend. She was very down to earth, and we always had respect for each other. We would have our moments and be in our mood or feelings, but we would talk it out and always come back together. It is not always easy living with female roommates, but you must learn how to respect each other's boundaries and give them space when needed.

The second semester of my senior year, I stayed in the Spartan suites. The Spartan Suites is like an apartment complex where you get to have your own room. I stayed in the suites with 3 other young ladies. I was excited to finally have my own room again, and not have to share. I did have to share a bathroom, but I did not mind that because I was used to that by now. There were two rooms on each floor with a bathroom in the middle. It was a cool set up. I almost forgot how it felt to have a room all to myself. I also had to share the kitchen space, but I did not mind sharing the space because I got to go back to my room alone! After all I have been through so much with roommates, I finally enjoyed and appreciated having a room to myself.

As far as my dorm mates, I really did not talk to them as much because I mostly stayed to myself. I already had a group of friends that I hung out with, so I was content with my routine. We had respect for each other and everyone's personal space, so I was grateful for that. What I learned about roommates throughout my college experience was, not everyone is going to be your friend, and that everyone is not going to agree or get along with you. For the most part, I had good times surrounding dorm life. I enjoyed my senior year in the Spartan Suites the most because there was no roommate, and I was just about done with college. I could not believe it, but I made it through. Thank God!

First College Dance

I went to my first college dance with a couple of girls I met in Midrise Dorms. I think this was my first official weekend staying on campus in a long time because I would usually go home for the weekend. The dance was on a Saturday night at Echols Hall in the gym at NSU. I remember I got dressed and put on my blue jeans with a cute red shirt. I got a text from the girls to meet them in the lobby, and for us to head out to the gym. I got my purse and started walking out to the lobby. I was extra nervous because I am not a person who goes out a lot, and I knew I had to socialize. We got to the gym, stood in line, then showed our ID's to get in. When we got into the gym, it was already packed with students dancing. I followed the girls into the crowd, and we found a spot to stand in. The girls started dancing with people and I watched them because I do not really dance. They were having fun and I cheered them on. The music was loud, and it was ridiculously hot in the gym.

I got bumped a lot as you can imagine me trying to keep my crutches out of the way. It was almost impossible because it was so crowded. It was annoying! Aside from it being crowded, some were not paying attention to where they were going. To avoid someone from tripping and/or falling, I decided to head over to the wall and chill there. Right before I got there, a boy from the dance floor walked up on me and just started to dance. Let us just say I never made it to the wall. He really helped my night to shift for the better. I had a lot of fun, but at the end of the night I was paying for it. My feet were hollering cats and dogs. Ha-ha!!! My feet hurt so bad. I had to rest a little before I took that walk back to my room.

The girls I came with texted me and said they were ready to go, so we walked out together and went back to the dorm. I took a shower and collapsed in the bed. That night was the best night of my freshman year. All the other dances I attended during my four years in college, I stood up against the wall in the gym and watched everyone else have a good time. I noticed being in crowds made me too nervous, and to add crutches to the situation made it even worse. It seemed like people never paid attention and ended up bumping me! That was not much fun. I had to focus on my balance, and people bumping into me stressed me out. I was afraid of falling. The bottom of my crutches would lose grip and get all slippery from the sweat on the floors from people dancing. It was hard to have fun and dance when your crutch grip is sliding. Ha-ha.

I did enjoy myself at the dance, but I just thought it would be best for me to stay away from those crowds because most of the students were drunk or wilding out when they were dancing. Just trying to have a conversation at the dance was even harder.

Sometimes the music would be so loud that you could not even hear yourself talk Ha-ha. So no, I was not being antisocial during school dances, I was being careful. Anxiety used to tell me to run away and sit down, but not anymore. I wanted to join the crowd and dance, but I kind of felt like this disability limited me from doing that. All in all, I had people to hang with at the dances and that is what mattered the most.

Chapter 6

First in Line

Chapter 6
First in Line

Some people may think that putting emphasis on being on time is not a big deal, but it is important to me. You may have even heard some people refer to being late as "colored (CP) time" because the misconception is that they are always late or even start events late. Time is precious and we can never get it back, so I value every moment. I always must be conscious of time because it could make life easy or hard for me. Being on time or even early helps me to reserve the seat I want/need, beat the crowd, or even get first pick of things. For me, running late does not work in my favor because I need extra time to do most things, so time management is essential for me with this disability.

I remember a homecoming concert at my college, I was excited to go to. I can still see that day in my mind. I had to go to my classes on a Wednesday and I was already tired from the long day. I really wanted to skip my art class that was towards the end of the day, but my professor already warned us not to. He told us a week prior that points would be deducted from our grade if we did not attend his class on the day of the homecoming concert.

He must have experienced empty classes around homecoming before. Ha-ha. After class, I headed back to my dorm to get ready for the homecoming concert. The performer for the concert was a well-known artist, so I knew the concert would be packed at capacity.

The walk back to my dorm took about 15 minutes because the Performance Art building was nearly in the back of the campus from where I stayed in the Midrise dorm towards the front. That is a long walk for someone like me with crutches. After finally making it to my room, I took a shower and put on this cute grey dress. I had to constantly keep track of time because I had to be there early to get a good seat. Not only do I walk with crutches but I am on the shorter side, 4"11 to be exact. It would be harder for me to see anything from the back. I was finally ready, so out the door I went.

I walked to Echols Hall where the concert would be, and no one was in line yet. That is the way I like it because I wanted to be first in line. Mind you, the concert did not start until 8:00pm, but the doors open at 7:30pm. I arrived around 6:00pm. I know that might sound crazy to some, but I must always take this disability into consideration. I do not walk as fast as the next person, nor can I stand up that long, so when I sit down, I want to still be able to see. Timing is particularly important to me and I did not play around with it. One small delay can mess up my whole day. Some understood this about me, but most did not and that was okay. I just had to stay focused on what is best for me. People started arriving to the line around 6:30pm. I saw some of the girls that I would socialize with from time to time, so I began to talk with them to pass time. We had a good time, but I would always think to myself, "do they really know what it's like to be forced to go the extra mile?" If I had it my way, I would have just showed up when the concert started! Instead, I had to arrive extra early and wait.

I wish my friends and I could have gone to homecoming concerts together, but our timing never worked out. Either they did not want to go, or they did not want to leave as early as I had to. I needed to be first in line and could not allow them to jeopardize that for me. If I waited for them, I would always end up in the back not being able to see anything in life. I just had to step out on faith and believe everything would work out for my good because my due diligence was not in vain.

They finally opened the doors for the concert, and I was able to walk to the front of the stage. They had a gate blocking off the main stage. Therefore, I was able to put my crutches over the metal gate and hold onto the gate for better support during the concert. This was a concert that you had to stand up the whole time unless you wanted to sit down on the bleachers in the gym. I did not want to sit in the gym after I waited all that time in line.

Besides, I wanted to interact with the crowd and the bleachers were more isolated at a distance.

Time flew and before I knew it the concert was over. I really enjoyed the homecoming concert and I think it was the best concert I have ever experienced. Yes, I got bumped here and there because it was a tight space with lots of people, but I enjoyed myself. Also, standing on my feet all night made me tired, but once the music started playing and the performers came on stage my body forgot all about the tiredness. The only thing I regret that day was not eating before the concert! Ha-ha. I was in a hurry all that day and did not have time to eat.

With back-to-back classes that day, I had no time to even get my thoughts together. I did not want to lose my place in line, so I took my chances. Boy oh boy was I hungry after the concert!

Thankfully, my roommate took me to a cookout after the concert. This was just one example of being on time or should I say being first in line. I always had to plan for different events in college. I enjoyed the football and basketball games, so I had to arrive early just to get a good seat. I had to start my journey at least 30 minutes ahead of time just to beat the crowd. I needed to be waiting by the doors before they opened.

I could not even leave with my friends because they would want to arrive at the last minute. They did not care about sitting in the front, but I did. My comfort was depending on it. Dealing with crowds and finding a seat on the first or second row is hard to do when you are late. Therefore, I am so adamant about time. I went early to events on campus because I was guaranteed to find me a good seat on the floor. I could not go up a lot of stairs with my crutches. If I went to events alone, I had to think about holding on to my crutches and going up one or two steps to sit down.

That is why being on time was essential because I wanted to be able to sit down and get myself together before the crowd came.

It was always something I had to work at. I was used to going the extra mile, so taking control of my schedule was nothing! I just hated that it felt like time was not on my side, and I was in a hurry more times than not. I wanted to just be able to take a moment to stop and smell the roses.

Rainy days in College

I want to take some time to talk about the rainy days at Norfolk State University. There were plenty rainy days at NSU, and I had to learn how to maneuver around campus when it would pour down raining. It was a big chore just trying to go from class to class. Looking back over my freshman year of college, I almost did not make it because of the rain. I would want to stay in bed during the rainy days, but too many days missed from class would result in them withdrawing me from the class. I could not afford that. I began taking the shuttle bus and that seemed as if it took decades to arrive at each stop. By the time the bus came I was tired from standing and for some reason the rain was colder than not. I would hate it when I would have to look for a seat on the bus after the front row was filled because I would usually sit in the front.

Even the process just to get on the bus was a lot. I needed the bus driver to take my crutches so that I could hold on to the rail and walk up the steps on the bus. Then the bus driver would hand my crutches back to me when I got to my seat. Well, here is a disclaimer. This was not how the bus ride went each time because some of the bus drivers were a little lazy and did not want to help me. I would have to manage my crutches and maintain my balance while I walked to my seat without any help. It would make me upset at times, but I guess it was not their job to help me although it would have been nice. I do not think I would have done that to anyone. I guess not everyone is like me. I do not mind helping anyone. If it is in my power, I would go the extra mile for the next person. I am grateful for all the bus drivers that wanted to help me. Imagine trying to keep your balance while walking up steps with your hands full, well that was me when I did not receive any help. It was scary because I did not want to fall. Some days I would be so frustrated because getting around the campus was the main thing I worried about! I was used to always having help, to now having to do it all on my own. By the time I became a sophomore, I learned how to make it to my classes in the rain without riding that shuttle bus.

I got better with preparing myself for rainy days by looking through my weather app on my phone to plan out my days for the week. I got a durable rain jacket with a nice big hood and a hat to cover me in the rain. I also, got a backpack with 3 different compartments so that I could put my books in two compartments and my jacket in the other. If I had extra space, my lunch would go there, so I was prepared to maneuver in the rain.

I know that most of you will read this and say wow, that was a lot to think about just to walk to class in the rain, but this is my life every day! It is all frustrating and overwhelming at times. A lot of it was trial and error trying to figure out what works best for me. I would see my roommate's sleep in on rainy days with no care in the world, but I would have to go through a whole routine just to make it to class. I valued my education, so I was not just going to miss class because it was raining. I had to continue going the extra mile even if I did not want to. The last thing I want to hear is someone without a disability complaining about getting to class in the rain and on time! If I can do it with all that I go through, then I know the next person can.

Chapter 7

NSU Childcare Internship

Chapter 7
<u>NSU Childcare Internship</u>

When most people go into their senior year, they are looking forward to graduate and enjoy their last year of school. Well, for me my senior year was not that great. Let me tell you about the start of my internship at Norfolk State University. I remember going into the NSU Child Development Lab to talk to the program director Ms. Rose about the start of my internship for my senior year. What I thought was going to be a great meeting ended up going downhill. When I sat down with her in her office, she began telling me about the internship and what I would be doing on a weekly to daily basis. I was going to observe the children in the class and work with the teachers in the classroom.

The meeting was going fine until she asked me personal questions that had no relevance towards the internship. I felt she was more worried about my disability then what I could do. Ms. Rose asked me questions such as, why did I pick Early Childhood Education as my career? I told her I picked it because I loved working with children. Her tone changed with me and everything she said was negative. She began telling me it was going to be hard to find work in my field because nobody would be willing to hire me. I felt my whole body shut down in disappointment as she was talking to me. I just heard a bunch of rambling coming from her mouth because my mind was not allowing the words to penetrate my mind. I was so shocked because the last thing I wanted to worry about was if the years I spent in school were all in vain. I chose the major I did because I wanted to help children, not just graduate to say I did it.

She could not understand, or shall I say would not understand how I could work with children while having a disability. She wanted to know how I would get around the classroom. She then asked if I had anything to say, but I just held my peace. I was furious with the questions that she had asked. At the end of the interview, she seemed frustrated and told me she had to sit down with the director of the program to see what they wanted to do with me. I was confused as to what she meant by that, but I am sure it was a nice way of telling me they did not want me to intern with them. You better believe I was pissed off with her and over that interview!

Imagine hearing someone putting you down because of a disability. I felt so ashamed and embarrassed. This program director had known me since freshman year of college. She had seen me do my hours in the lab where I would observe the children and interact with them! She had the audacity to act like she never knew who I was nor remembered seeing me do my required hours. I remember being done with the interview and holding my tears back as I got up from the chair. I put on my book bag, got my crutches, then walked out. When I walked out the door, I remember telling myself to calm down because my heart was racing fast. I walked into the public restroom and broke down in tears. I called my dad and told him I just wanted to come home.

After my break down in the bathroom I walked back to the suites and told my best friend what was said in the meeting. I finally got to my room and laid down on the bed. I really was analyzing my life, thoughts, and actions. My dad ended up going to the school to talk to the dean because he was upset about what the childcare director said to me. He was extremely mad and wanted to meet with the top administrators. The dean told us that she would have a meeting with faculty and staff. The meeting would consist of faculty from School of Education, the disability office, and faculty from Childcare Development Lab. I remember walking into the conference room for the meeting nervous and I sat down next to my dad. During the meeting, my dad read a letter that my mom had written stating that they were disappointed in how the Director of the childcare center had treated me. The letter also stated that they had higher expectations because I attended a HBCU. They expected me to be able to get a good education and become successful after I graduated. They felt as if I was being let down by some of the faculty on campus. Once my dad finished reading the letter there was not a dry eye in sight. Faculty members at the table all seemed moved by the letter that my dad read. That meeting was a moment in history, and I will never forget the speechlessness I witnessed in the room that day. You could hear a pin drop because everyone was silent. I thank God for justice and for bottling up my tears to grow something beautiful.

Chapter 8

NSU Graduation

Chapter 8
NSU Graduation

Walking across the stage during my graduation was one of the most significant moments of my life. I received my bachelor's degree from Norfolk State University. Have you ever imagined yourself accomplishing a critical goal in your life but was nervous about how it would play out? Well, that day had finally come true for me. My undergrad graduation was on May 7, 2016.

That day was unforgettable! It all started when I first arrived at the Norfolk Scope with my family for graduation. The morning started kind of rushed and hectic when my mom, sister and I walked back to the dressing room, we were stopped by a man at the front door. My dad had taken my grandmothers to the arena to be seated. My mom started to get upset as she was telling the man we were family, and that she needed to help me with my graduation cap and gown. The man checked with the staff to see if my mom could join me although he had an attitude. He then told her she could finally come in with me, but my sister could not join us, so she waited for my mom outside the arena.

As my mom helped me put on my cap and gown, all my peer's backstage was excited and celebrating! I remember having to get in line to get my name tag for graduation. As I was getting situated, the advisor helping with the graduation told my mother she would help me across the stage. I was grateful that she wanted to help me walk across the stage. I was ready to receive my degree that I put so much hard work into. As time grew closer to walk out to our seats, we all began to line up with our assigned groups. I was assigned to the Early Childhood Education group because that was my major. I was so nervous and could feel my heart beating through my chest. I remember the faculty shouting at us to get in line correctly and to keep our voices down.

As we started walking out to our seats, I could hear the President of Norfolk State University talking to the people in the crowd on the loudspeaker. I became even more nervous. As my group was walking out, I began to see the people in the stands. I was so frazzled with my heart beating extra fast that I thought I was going to pass out. I scanned the crowd to see if I could spot my family, and after tediously searching, I spotted them. They were standing on the right side of the arena in the front section of the stands. I felt my whole body go into shock as I looked at them, waving, smiling, and shouting my name. I could see the love and happiness on their faces. It was at that very moment I felt all my hard work had paid off from school. All the late nights of staying up studying, writing papers, learning how to be independent, and to do things on my own. During my four years of college, I had gotten so much stronger as an individual, and I thank God for that. I felt empowered and ready to conquer the world.

As I sat down in my seat for graduation, I remember looking at all my family members and smiling with joy. The ceremony had begun, and the speaker for our ceremony began to speak. I could not tell you everything the man was talking about because I was worried about making sure I had someone to hold my crutches as I walked up the steps to get my degree. My mind was solely focused on not tripping and falling on the biggest day of my life. After the speaker was done talking to us, it was time to stand in line and walk to the front of the stage to get our degrees. As I saw my peers walking up to get their degree's one by one, I remember asking my friend if she could help me by holding my crutches while I walked up the stairs and making sure she handed them back to me once I got to the top. She was very calm and reassuring that she was there to help with whatever I needed her to do. I always had to have a backup plan in my head because I have been let down too many times. As I learned throughout my college years, if you want something done, you must do it yourself even if you must constantly go the extra mile. I had no one to count on, but myself and God at the end of the day. I was glad I finally made it through college!

When it was my turn to go upfront, I remembered faculty members hugging me and telling me how proud they were of all my accomplishments. They seemed so happy with tears in their eyes as I thanked each one of them. I finally reached the center of the stage, and the photographer stopped me to ask if he could take a picture of me in my cap and grown. I was so grateful and honored that he would ask me for a picture because he did not ask everyone. I allowed him to take my picture and he began snapping pictures left and right of me. I was smiling so hard that my face started to hurt. Ha-ha. After he was done, it was my turn to get my degree. The moment I have been waiting for my whole life was right before my very eyes! I had so many emotions happen at once that I could see stars for a second. Even if I passed out, I was going to get back up and still receive my degree in my hand.

I almost forgot I had to give the announcer my name card so that she could say my name over the speaker. I gave the announcer my name card and all I could recall was my full name being called out loud, then hearing my family members yelling my name from the stands. It felt so unreal! I had walked across the stage and shook the President of Norfolk State University's hand as he held my degree. The photographer appeared in front of me again to take a picture of the President and I, as I held my degree. The faculty member that was assisting me held my degree for me as I walked to my seat because I could not hold it and my crutches at the same time. I had to go down the steps to get off the stage as the next person was being called to get their degree. Of course, I had to give my crutches up so I could hold onto the railing. I really pray every day that some miracle breakthrough would happen to heal me, so I do not have to go through the extra stuff anymore! This was an amazing day for me thus far, so I tried my hardest not to focus on the process I had to go through just to get to and from my seat! Before I could get back to my seat, I had to take an official graduation picture with my degree with another photographer. I made it to my seat and was greeted by my family. They were celebrating me and taking pictures.

The faculty member helping me handed me my Early Childhood Education degree and I began to shed tears of joy. I felt a sense of peace and relief because I was an official graduate. I made it back to my seat safely without tripping or falling on stage because that was my biggest fear. Ha-ha!! I sat there thinking how proud I was of myself. I did it! I did it! I did it! Yes, I did it! At the end of the graduation, everyone turned their tassel to the other side of their graduation cap. Everyone clapped and jumped for joy as we were overwhelmed with excitement. When we were released from the ceremony, we all had to walk backstage to grab our belongings and meet up with our families. Walking backstage felt great because I was officially an alumnus of Norfolk State University. As I was leaving out the building and taking last minute pictures with my family, I remember people coming up to me telling me how proud they were of me.

This one man stopped me and said I was an inspiration to him, and he admired my strength. He said once he saw me walk across the stage, he realized that he was complaining about little things in life. He realized he could do whatever he wanted if he believed in himself. Hearing that melted my heart and that let me know that people see how hard I have work to reach my goal and what I have accomplished. I also went back to school in August of 2016 to receive my Master's in Professional School Counseling. I received my master's degree in December of 2018. That was also one of the best days of my life: to walk across the stage a second time to receive my master's degree. I know it was only God that got me through.

Chapter 9

After College and Coming Home

Chapter 9
Home After College

When I moved out of the suites on campus and returned home to do my internships for my master's degree, I fell into a deep depression. It was not going the way I wanted it to. I had to adjust being away from school and hanging out with people that I did not know. I regret not being able to do my internship at school because I think it would have been easier in an environment I had already adjusted to.

While I did my internship at home, I practiced driving so I could be able to drive myself around. I eventually got the hang of it and was able to drive myself to the nail shop to get my nails done. I feel like my driving has improved tremendously since I graduated from college. It might not mean much to some but being able to independently drive myself around meant the world to me. Plus, I was able to get my nails done on the regular and grab some delicious food from my favorite spots. Being able to drive is a big deal for me and it makes me feel good about myself. I love the fact that I have mastered driving and have the freedom to go wherever I want.

It has been a year and a half since I have been home, and I must say that it gets boring and depressing with nothing to do. Depression hit me hard after I graduated in December of 2018 from NSU with my master's degree. My mom would go to work and my dad worked from home, so they were occupied. I felt like no one understood how I was feeling or what I was going through. I no longer had my college friends because we all went our separate ways, so I was left to hang out alone again. I already knew how to be alone, I guess it was a matter of me just doing it. I thought I was past that stage in life. If only I could keep consistent friends! Until then, I just had to be my own best friend. My sister was in college getting her undergrad degree, so I did not want to call her every day to bother her. Or at least I felt like a bother because I knew she needed to focus on her schoolwork instead of talking to me. I had to figure out how to cope with this transition in life. I eventually started hanging out with my cousin and doing things with her. We went to concerts, movies, and nice restaurants. She always made me feel included and wanted. She even invited me to several of her friend's parties and other events. She made me feel loved, and I am very appreciative of that. My best friend just so happens to be my cousin.

I have seen a lot of my peers go on to have families and enjoy life with their significant other. I just pray when the time is right God sends me a husband that I can enjoy life with. I know my cousin does her best to make time for me, but I know at some point she will not have time for me anymore. I hate being lonely and all by myself. People have told me that I do not understand "adult life" because I do not have a family of my own, but I beg to differ. Every day I picture my own family in my head, and I have already mapped out a life for us. I know how to love them and will ask God to lead me in everything, that will be all that matters.

Social media does not help when I am feeling alone because I look and only see happy faces. It only reminds me that I am still by myself. Ha-ha. Sometimes I feel like I have no purpose in life because I feel empty inside. I have my wonderful family that I am very thankful for, but I pray for purpose each and every day.

Chapter 10

Searching for Jobs

Chapter 10
Searching for Jobs

After I graduated college with my master's in counseling, I was excited to start job searching. Little did I know it was not going to be a walk in the park. I started looking for professional counseling jobs thinking they would see that I had a master's and hire me right away, but that was not the case. I remember my first job interview at Creekside Elementary School. That is where I did my second internship for my master's degree. I was excited because, I had just finished my internship and I felt I had a good chance at receiving the school's counselor position. I remember walking into the interview ready to answer all the questions. When I went in the conference room the Principal of Creekside was there along with one other staff member. I was so nervous, because this was my first interview, I had done for a job position. When the principal started asking me questions, I started to freeze up because I did not know all the answers. I thought I was going to ace this interview, but I started second guessing it. She asked me about 10 questions during the interview.

I knew after the interview that I was not going to get that counseling position. Within the next couple of weeks, I received an email saying that the position had been filled. I was disappointed, but I did not get to upset because it was my first interview. I continued to move forward and kept applying for jobs. I kept applying for school counseling positions in the surrounding areas. I kept getting denied. I got so tired of looking through my emails telling me that the position had been filled! It really started to annoy me. As I sat in the lobby waiting to be interviewed, the principal would come out calling my name with excitement, but as soon as they saw me their whole demeanor would change. They would shake my hand and rush through the interview so they could go on to the next. Before the interview even started, they already made up their minds that I was not the best candidate for the position. I felt in my heart that they were biased, discriminative, and even judgmental when they saw me walk in with crutches. When I did my interviews, I would not always come out and say that I have cerebral palsy because I felt it was no one's business to know. After a while, I just got tired of repeating myself and even going the extra mile to impress these people in the interview. I felt if my bachelor's and/or master's degree did not speak for themselves, then I did not need to be there. After my last interview in 2019 when the principal of an elementary school told me she would call me back to let me know if I had the job, I gave up because I knew at that very moment, I did not get it. That position was for a teacher's assistant and they were hiring like crazy. I got an email in the next couple of days saying you know what, "the position had been filled." I thought to myself maybe school counseling was not for me. I would think to myself why did I even go to school to get a master's in school counseling? I truly felt I wasted two years of my life for nothing.

Job searching made me rethink my future. I have not looked for a job since covid-19 began. I have been thinking about looking for jobs in social work instead and even going back to school to get a second master's degree. I want to investigate substance abuse counseling as well. Those are two fields I am extremely interested in and would like to find a job in those areas. As far as school counseling, I have not fully given up on getting a position. I just know I cannot keep applying solely for that position. I want to step out of the box and try looking into other careers that I have interest in as well. It is hard getting a job anyway since people look at me as less than because of this disability. Imagine people judging you off your appearance, well that is the story of my life! Since I use crutches to walk, they immediately think my brain does not work. They even view me as a little child because I'm 4"11 and look young for my age. When in fact, I am a thirty-year-old young woman who is trying to make her way in this world. I am just trying to fully live independently, and it will be hard to do that without a job or career.

Since the job search has been off to a rough start, I must figure out a different way to make a living for myself. I hope this book will give people insight on my life and the issues that I deal with daily. I hope in the future someone will step out on faith and give me a position. I made a vision board because my therapist told me it would help me plan. Some of the jobs I listed were social worker, substance abuse counselor, and creative writer. I would be interested in one of those careers for the future.

My biggest dream on the vision board was to work with Tyler Perry and be in some of his movies or plays. I would love to get in the industry and be an actress. I know that is kind of reaching, but it is my dream to be able to accomplish that. His movies and plays are special to me. When I watch his movies and plays, they make me feel happy. I feel a burning desire igniting. Maybe that is what I am really supposed to be doing in life, but I settled with a counseling degree. I got BET Plus movie app just to watch Tyler Perry plays and movies over and over. But hey, nothing is wrong with a girl dreaming, right? I just hope that one day I would be able to make a living for myself and be able to live a life that I desire in my heart.

Chapter 11

My Faith

Chapter 11
My Faith

I was born and raised in a Christian household. When I was younger, I went to my grandmother's church called New Cavalry Baptist Church. Both of my grandmothers taught me the Word of God. I used to love going to church and seeing the people in the seats smiling as they heard the Word being preached. I could not quite understand everything that the pastor talked about when I was younger, but I was glad to be there with my family.

As I got older, I started to understand the Word of God and wanted to learn more. My faith was not always the best growing up as a teenager because my emotions were always all over the place. I would question why God gave me this disability and why I could not be normal like everyone else. Why did I have to go through the hardships of life and always go the extra mile? I know they say not to question God, but did God say that? Or did we just make that up? I believe we should be able to ask our Heavenly Father anything, but it is up to Him to answer us of course. I look at it the same way I would ask my earthly dad a question. I do not mean any harm or disrespect; I would just like to know why He picked me to have cerebral palsy.

My faith was always up and down. I wanted to have more faith in God because I know He has power to do anything. It was all just a matter of me believing what I knew. It is crazy once you think about it. I know something, but do not believe it? I know that I believe God exist, but I always doubt within myself that God loves me because of this disability that hunts me. I even wonder if He hears my prayers that I say every night. I would question if I were praying correctly because I did not know all the scriptures in the bible. I felt as if I did not really know how to talk to God since I do not know the Bible from front to back. I finally realized that all you must do is be truthful and just talk to God from your heart. He hears you no matter if He answers your prayers or not. Not every prayer lines up with His Will for your life, so it will not happen. My struggle is all part of my purpose and I must learn how to embrace that.

I really started to understand the Word of God better when we started attending Grove Church. When I first visited that church one Sunday morning, I was shocked to witness how much love and happiness they showed to us. It just felt good to hear the choir singing songs and the people felt like family. It was a heartwarming experience. When I heard the pastor preach, I felt as though I could understand the Word of God better. It was so refreshing to me. He spoke with so much passion and love for the Word of God. I knew in my heart that I wanted to return to that church repeatedly because I finally found a preacher that I could relate too. My family and I ended up becoming members of that church and have been enjoying their services ever since. I just love how the pastor extends himself to the people and the community.

In college, my faith grew through the roof the duration of time that I was there because I needed God like never before. It was just Him and I. I prayed every single day! I tell you what, God got my attention during my college years because I was always in need of Him. I realize I cannot make it in this life without Him. I owe Him my life because He kept me even when I wanted to take my life. I prayed and still pray to Him every night because I dealt with a whole lot in college just with the roommates alone!

When I tell you God pulled me through, it is not nothing but the truth. I had to learn how to depend on God and know that He will get me through anything. With His grace and mercy, I got my bachelor's degree and my master's degree. I tell you all this to say, that sometimes God must put you in an uncomfortable space for you to hear Him. I am nowhere near perfect and my faith has not always been strong, but I continue to allow God to work on me every single day. I strive to please God because in the end that is all that will be accounted for. I used to be upset with God for making me disabled, but I now know everything has a purpose even this.

Chapter 12

Dating

Chapter 12
<u>Dating</u>

I had my first official boyfriend in College. I met him my sophomore year at NSU. I met him in the childhood development lab. I was observing him for some time in class but too nervous to say anything. He was a football player for NSU. He was such a nice young man. In the beginning of the relationship everything was going well. He spent time with me and took me out on dates. He was an upcoming rapper and would invite me to his shows. I thought this relationship was what I wanted and had prayed for, but it was not. Looking back now, I do not think I was fully prepared for a relationship. He accepted me with cerebral palsy and all. I was so grateful for that. Being in a relationship required a lot of work such as communication and patience. Sometimes I would shut down because I felt like he would unintentionally push me to do things I had no interest in doing.

I was young and just started accepting the demands of college. To be honest, I was not used to getting attention like that. I did not want to be tied down in a relationship then because it was unforeseen work that I did not have time for. I did not feel like explaining myself or doing things out of my comfort zone. My thoughts were, I would rather be alone than to deal with someone else's personality at that point in my life. Worrying about someone else at that time took a toll on me. After a while, I just wanted to be friends, but he wanted to be in ma serious relationship. We ended up breaking up. I was upset about how our relationship ended to be honest. It was over something so silly. As time went on, I enjoyed being by myself and just hanging out with my roommates as we enjoyed campus life.

I am much older now and out of college and sometimes I wish I would have held on to that relationship. I think the only reason I wanted to get back into the relationship, was just to say I have someone. I thought it might help fill the void of loneliness. That is the only reason I would have gone back to the relation because I hate being lonely.

Dating after college

Dating after college has not been easy. Sometimes I would rather deal with myself than to deal with someone else's baggage. I have not given up on love, sometimes I am just not in the mood for some reason. Plus, it is a lot to deal with even though I do want a relationship. I just have not run across the right one yet. I pray that when I do, it will be a relationship designed just for me. I am more of the traditional girl. I want the guy I am interested in to meet my parents. I do not want it to be forced. I want him to be willing. I want him to be able to look pass cerebral palsy and see me for who I am. I want him to love all of me because of who I am and not out of pity. I want him to accept me for better or for worst and even my ups and downs. I want fulfillment in every way. I have this thing where I push people away before they push me away, so I pray that he is strong enough to get through to me when I want to run. I pray he is persistent and consistent in all that he does and speak. I want to be loved beyond what is seen. I want him to fall in love with my mind, my smile, and my funny jokes. I do not want him to ever grow tired of me. I want us to hold hands forever. I know God is working on my behalf, and it is just a matter of me being patient and trusting Him every day. I know when God's name is on something, He made it good, so I will wait for God to reveal Mr. Right. I am no longer going to worry about the fact that I walk with crutches because if the guy is God sent, he will be able to look past that.

I get jealous sometimes when I see others in relationships, and I am still in the waiting room. Many ask me why I am still single at thirty years old, but I guess God wants me to wait a little longer. Some people even think I am gay because I am up in age with no man. Ha-ha. This new generation is not like the one back in the day when I was younger. I have a hard time getting out of my head sometimes. I feel like this disability is ruining my life. I feel it is in the way of my love life, career, friends, etc. I am grateful for the few that accept me, but I want more! I pray God hears the cry in my heart and comes through quickly, because He is the only reason, I take another step each day. He is the air that I breathe, and I know I cannot make it without Him. So, for right now I will leave my love life in God's hands and stay focused on Him.

Chapter 13

Happy Moments in my Life

Chapter 13
Happy Times in my life

One of the happiest times is my life was my 18th birthday party that my parents threw for me. It was also my cousin's big day because she was graduating from college with her degree in accounting. I remember waking up early and getting myself ready for the day. My mom and dad were organizing things for my party. My mom and dad got someone to perform for the celebration. The performer's name was Romonta.

My family and friends attended my party. We had tents and tables set up, a professional DJ, a caterer, and a professional performer. I believe it was about 60 to 70 people at my party. We had a whole plethora of food to serve the guests. We had chicken, pork chops, ribs, mac and cheese, and green beans. The weather was nice, and everyone was enjoying themselves. My family and friends celebrated my cousin and I on our joint celebration. Later that evening Romonta performed for us. We love all his music, and he treated my cousin and I like superstars!

Romonta autographed his poster for me and I still have the poster sitting in my room.

The party went on all night long because nobody wanted to leave. We all were eating, drinking, and enjoying the night. When it was time for the DJ to leave the party, my dad's best friend paid the DJ to stay a little longer. Ha-ha. It was a very wonderful and happy time in my life. The DJ was awesome! He played a mix of music for the young and older folks.

Romonta and his crew had a nice time with my family and friends. They were down to earth and very inviting. They spoke to most of my family at the party and had wonderful conversations with them. You would have thought they were part of the family. The crew left the party with plates full of good food. I was overwhelmed and full of joy because a professional music artist and his crew came to my party and performed for us. I had such a good time with my family. This was the first time I had ever experienced a professional music artist right in the comfort of my own back yard.

B2K Experience 2019

March 17, 2019 was another great day of my life. I got to go to the B2K experience concert, and I was lucky enough to have gotten two front row tickets!!!! I went to the concert with my God sister. This was an incredibly special concert because B2K's music group had been broken up for some years and I was a little sad about it when it happened, but they decided to do one last project together. They decided to do a world tour together and it was a big deal. I was so excited because I had a Meet and Greet ticket for the concert. I was able to go backstage to meet the group! I was so blown away to have gotten these tickets because this was finally my chance to meet all the members of B2K. I love all the members of the group Omarion, J-Boog, Raz- B, and Lil Fizz, but my favorite out the group is Omarion.

However, my day started like this, I got dressed in my cute little black top that had the words "Hustle" on it and my black leggings that had rips in it. I was so excited and remember taking selfies in the mirror in my cute outfit. As I finished getting ready, my God sister was pulling up to pick me up for the concert. She walked in the house with a cute pink dress on and a long flowing blonde wig. We both looked good. We started making our way to the front door as my mom made sure I had everything before we left. I was so happy to walk out to the car so we could be on our way to the concert. Driving to the Hampton Coliseum, I remember listening to music and just talking about how excited I was to meet the group.

We arrived at the Hampton Coliseum and I just remember seeing so many young people walking into the arena. As we walked in, we had to stand in line to get our Meet and Greet tickets. Once we got out tickets, we decided to get a snack before we went into the concert. It was people everywhere. I had to make sure that I took my time so I would not trip or fall. When I walk in crowds' people do not look down to see me because I am short. Yes, crowds are difficult for me because people are always bumping into me and not paying attention to where they are walking. We made it to our front row seats and sat down. I could not believe it! We were in the front row so I would be able to see everything and not have to worry about being knocked down by a bunch of females. There was even security posted in front of the stage to keep order. I felt a little relieved that they were there, so my protection was not a worry. The beginning of the concert had opening acts that performed before B2K went forward.

The performers were Mario, Pretty Ricky, Lloyd, Bobby V, Ying Yang Twins, and Chingy. When it was time for B2K to come on stage to perform, I jumped out of my seat as my heart was pumping fast from all the excitement that was going on in the arena. This was finally the moment I had dreamt of!!!

The group joining back together and doing a reunion tour for us fans was a dream come true. I dreamt of this moment probably as soon as they announced they were breaking up. They had solo careers, but it just was not the same as when they were together.

B2K did an amazing job performing that night. It was a night I would never forget. I was screaming and yelling the lyrics to the song all night. Omarion looked so good on stage! I wish I could have him all to myself. Picture that, him singing to only me. He was so dreamy that I could not take my eyes off him. He had my focus until the performance was over. I felt so much joy and happiness that night because I am truly one of their biggest fans. It felt amazing to have young people come together to fill the arena. Everyone enjoying themselves singing and yelling the lyrics of all the songs. That feeling was indescribable and that is one of the reasons why I love concerts. My voice was just about gone before the concert was over because I had screamed the entire night. I love their songs. I am telling you if you missed the B2K reunion, you missed a great concert.

When the concert was over, my God sister and I waited for the crowd to leave out of the coliseum because I did not want to get pushed and shoved while walking with the crowd. When we got to the car in the parking lot you can imagine how hectic it was to get out of traffic just to go right across the street for the meet and greet. When we got to the convention center across the street, we were a little late for the meet & greet. We went inside the building and the security guard was standing outside the VIP after party section. He told us that the meet and greet was over and that we missed our opportunity to take pictures. My God sister asked if she could speak to the manger because I had spent a pretty penny to get the front row seats at the concert and the Meet and Greet passes. The security guard spoke to the manger and we were able to go inside the VIP after party. When we got inside the party, we stood by the bar and the bodyguard asked us our names so that he could go get Omarion and the rest of the group to take pictures with us.

was so excited to finally meet each group member for the first ime ever. The bodyguard told us to follow him to the DJ booth vhere we met Omarion and took a picture with him. My nerves vere so bad that my hands were shaking as I was trying to take a inapchat picture of Omarion and me. The picture came out nice. was so happy with my snapchat picture. I got to take pictures vith the rest of the band members as well such as J-Boog, Raz-3 and Lil Fizz. It was such a great experience getting to meet this voy band because never in my life did, I think I would get a chance to meet all of them in person. It was one of the best concerts' of 2019 hands down!!!

Chapter 14

My Family

Chapter 14
My Family

Family has always been important to me because they are an amazing support system that I am truly blessed to have. If you know me, then you must know that I love being around my family. I have a close relationship with family. We are known for having cookouts, family reunions, and going on family vacation trips in the summertime. My favorite family time spent is our summer vacations together. I have been to the Bahamas, Disney World, Las Vegas, Philadelphia, Canada, New York City, and New Orleans. Our family trips are a time for us to bond and just hang out with each other. We may fuss and argue during our family trips, but we always make great memories with each other.

I am thankful to have my family and being able to experience holidays with them such as Thanksgiving and Christmas because we can all come together and love on each other. Thanksgiving and Christmas dinner is packed with so much food for everyone to eat, such as mac and cheese, candy yams, my grandma favorite dish cheese potatoes, turkey, etc. It is also a time of laughter, getting closer to one another, and being vulnerable with each other more. I could go on and on, but overall, I just love spending quality time with my love ones. Having people around you that love you and support you is worth more than all the money in the world.

My family has been there for me ever since I was born. My parents always wanted the best for me, so they always made sure I had everything I needed. My family never looked at me like I was not capable of doing anything. In fact, they would always push me harder to make it to my full potential. I just want to give my family a special thank you. You have supported me, and your love never goes unnoticed. I am so blessed to have such a close-knit family that cares about me. I love you all!!!!!

Chapter 15

Future Goals

Chapter 16
Future Goals

My future goals are to be able to go on book tours, speaking engagements, and do seminars. I want to be able to speak to people all over the world. I want to meet people who have cerebral palsy just like me. I want people to know that anything is possible with God. You just must believe. I want to be able to one day start my own cerebral palsy foundation. I would like to start the foundation in my hometown which is Suffolk, Virginia. I want the foundation to be about uplifting one another, such as building your confidence, and your self-esteem. I want to have charity events for people who have cerebral palsy and help raise money for surgeries, braces, wheelchairs, crutches, etc. I want to be able to help families of people with cerebral palsy.

I want to have seminars for people who want to learn about the effects of cerebral palsy. This seminar would teach people to understand what disabled people go through, how to treat them better, and help others to change their perspective about disabled people. Often people without disabilities do not understand the extra mile a person with a disability has to go through. I believe that being able to hear from people with disabilities will give more informative insight.

I would love to have my own website where people could share their testimonies and be able to read different stories about people who have cerebral palsy from all over the world. I want people to be able to share their stories and be heard for once, because often I think I am the only one who has cerebral palsy and that is far from the truth. People are everywhere with cerebral palsy and it is nothing to be ashamed of.

The second thing I want to do is to be able to work on a production set with Mr. Tyler Perry. When I say I love all his movies and plays, I really do. I have seen just about every play and movie out there that he has produced. I would love to act in one of his movies or tv shows. I would also love to write a script or movie with him one day. Maybe he will purchase a copy of my book one day and turn it into a movie or play. It is my dream. I know it might sound silly, but I know with God anything is possible because I do believe.

Conclusion

Conclusion

I hope this book gives you insight on my life and what I have been through dealing with cerebral palsy. I hope that after reading this book, that you have gotten to know me for who I am and not what plagues me. I am a smart, determined, and independent young lady who just so happens to be fighting with cerebral palsy. I pray you see the world from my point of view and that I have brought awareness to how I view the world.

From dealing with depression in high school to maneuvering around college, I went through a lot just to get my bachelor's degree and master's degree while living on campus. The different trials and tribulations I went through almost took me out, but God was there to help me persevere through it all. I love and enjoy sharing some of the things I experience day to day in hopes that others would have more compassion towards disabled people. My life seems like a complex puzzle sometimes, but I am figuring it out each day little by little. I hope the next time you see someone or anybody with any type of disability you ask yourself are you just looking at their outer appearance and judging them or do you really see them for who they are on the inside. They are human with feelings also. After all I have shared, I just want to know, do you SEE ME?

Acknowledgment

I would like to give a special thank you to Michael Brooks, owner of KameraShy. He took the time to capture my vision for my photos used for this book. I especially love the image used for my book cover because it made it perfect. Even the photo I used for my author's bio was excellent because it reminded me of the beauty I have always had. Now, I can look at my book repeatedly when I need a reminder of who I am.

If you are in the Virginia area and need a fantastic photographer, contact Michael Brooks at KameraShy; email address:

Soulful757@gmail.com